SPAIN IN OUR HEARTS

ESPAÑA EN EL CORAZÓN

Also by Pablo Neruda from New Directions

THE CAPTAIN'S VERSES

RESIDENCE ON EARTH

PABLO NERUDA

SPAIN IN OUR HEARTS:

HYMN TO THE GLORIES OF THE PEOPLE AT WAR

ESPAÑA EN EL CORAZÓN:

HIMNO A LAS GLORIAS DEL PUEBLO EN LA GUERRA

Translated by Donald D. Walsh

A NEW DIRECTIONS

Pablo Neruda originally published *España en el corazón* in 1937, and later included it in the third volume of *Residencia en la tierra*, first published by New Directions in 1973, and reissued in 2004. For this edition of *Spain in Our Hearts*, minor corrections were made based on Volume I of Galaxia Gutenberg's 2001 edition of Neruda's *Obras completas*, edited by Hernán Loyola.

The preface, "My Book on Spain," is an excerpt from *Memoirs* by Pablo Neruda, translated by Hardie St. Martin. Translation copyright © 1977 by Farrar, Straus and Giroux, Inc. Reprinted by permission of Farrar, Straus and Giroux, LLC.

Manufactured in the United States of America
New Directions Books are printed on acid-free paper.
First published as a New Directions Bibelot in 2005
Published simultaneously in Canada by Penguin Books Canada Limited

Library of Congress Cataloging-in-Publication Data

Neruda, Pablo, 1904-1973.
   [España en el corazón. English & Spanish]
   Spain in our hearts : hymn to the glories of the people at war = España en el corazón : himno a las glorias del pueblo en guerra : 1936-1937 / Pablo Neruda ; translated by Donald D. Walsh.
      p. cm. — (A New Directions bibelot)
   ISBN 0-8112-1642-X (alk. paper)
   1. Spain—History—Civil War, 1936-1939—Poetry. I. Title: España en el corazón. II. Walsh, Donald Devenish, 1903-1980 III. Title. IV. Series.
   PQ8097.N4E79 2006
   861'.62—dc22
                                                              2005023640

New Directions Books are published for James Laughlin
by New Directions Publishing Corporation
80 Eighth Avenue, New York, NY 10011

CONTENTS

PREFACE:

"My Book on Spain" by Pablo Neruda   vii

ESPAÑA EN EL CORAZON
      SPAIN IN OUR HEARTS

Invocación / Invocation	2
Bombardeo / Bombardment	4
Maldición / Curse	4
España pobre por culpa de los ricos / Spain Poor Through the Fault of the Rich	4
La tradición / Tradition	6
Madrid (1936) / Madrid (1936)	8
Explico algunas cosas / I Explain a Few Things	10
Canto a las madres de los milicianos muertos / Song for the Mothers of Slain Militiamen	14
Cómo era España / What Spain Was Like	20
Llegada a Madrid de La Brigada Internacional / Arrival in Madrid of the International Brigade	26
Batalla del río Jarama / Battle of the Jarama River	30
Almería / Almería	32
Tierras ofendidas / Offended Lands	34
Sanjurjo en los infiernos / Sanjurjo in Hell	36

Mola en los infiernos / Mola in Hell   38

El general Franco en los infiernos /
   General Franco in Hell   38

Canto sobre unas ruinas / Song about Some Ruins   44

La victoria de las armas del pueblo /
   The Victory of the Arms of the People   46

Los gremios en el frente / The Unions at the Front   48

Triunfo / Triumph   48

Paisaje después de una batalla /
   Landscape After a Battle   50

Antitanquistas / Antitankers   50

Madrid (1937) / Madrid (1937)   54

Oda solar al Ejército del Pueblo /
   Solar Ode to the Army of the People   60

PREFACE:
"My Book on Spain" by Pablo Neruda

Time passed. We were beginning to lose the war. The poets sided with the Spanish people: Federico had been murdered in Granada. Miguel Hernández had been transformed from a goatherd into a fighting word. In soldier's uniform, he read his poems on the front lines. Manuel Altolaguirre kept his printing presses going. He set one up on the eastern front, near Gerona, in an old monastery. My book *España en el corazón* was printed there in a unique way. I believe few books, in the extraordinary history of so many books, have had such a curious birth and fate.

The soldiers at the front learned to set type. But there was no paper. They found an old mill and decided to make it there. A strange mixture was concocted, between one falling bomb and the next, in the middle of the fighting. They threw everything they could get their hands on into the mill, from an enemy flag to a Moorish soldier's bloodstained tunic. And in spite of the unusual materials used and the total inexperience of its manufacturers, the paper turned out to be very beautiful. The few copies of that book still in existence produce astonishment at its typography and at its mysteriously manufactured pages. Years later I saw a copy in the Library of Congress in Washington, D.C., displayed in a showcase as one of the rarest books of our time.

My book had just been printed and bound when the Republic's defeat was suddenly upon us. Hundreds of thousands of refugees glutted the roads leading out of Spain. It was the exodus, the most painful event in the history of that country.

Among those lines of people going into exile were the survivors of the eastern front, and with them Manuel Altolaguirre and the soldiers who had made the paper and printed *España en el corazón.* My book was the pride of these men who had worked to bring out my poetry in the face of death. I learned that many carried copies of the book in their sacks, instead of their own food and clothing. With those sacks over their shoulders, they set out on the long march to France.

The endless column walking to exile was bombed hundreds of times. Soldiers fell and the books were spilled on the highway. Others continued their interminable flight. On the other side of the border, the Spaniards who reached exile met with brutal treatment. The last copies of this impassioned book that was born and perished in the midst of fierce fighting were immolated in a bonfire.

Miguel Hernández sought refuge in the Chilean Embassy, which during the war had granted asylum to four thousand Franco followers. Carlos Morla Lynch, the ambassador, claimed to be his friend but denied the great poet his protection. A few days after, he was arrested and thrown into prison. He died of tuberculosis in jail three years later. The nightingale could not survive in captivity.

My consular duties had come to an end. Because I had taken part in the defense of the Spanish Republic, the Chilean government decided to remove me from my post.

from Neruda's Memoirs (1974), *translated by Hardie St. Martin*

SPAIN IN OUR HEARTS

HEARTS

ESPAÑA EN EL

CORAZÓN

INVOCACIÓN

Para empezar, para sobre la rosa
pura y partida, para sobre el origen
de cielo y aire y tierra, la voluntad de un canto
con explosiones, el deseo
de un canto inmenso, de un metal que recoja
guerra y desnuda sangre.
                    España, cristal de copa, no diadema,
sí machacada piedra, combatida ternura
de trigo, cuero y animal ardiendo.

Mañana, hoy, por tus pasos
un silencio, un asombro de esperanzas
como un aire mayor: una luz, una luna,
luna gastada, luna de mano en mano,
de campana en campana!
                    Madre natal, puño
de avena endurecida,
                    planeta
seco y sangriento de los héroes!
Quién? por caminos, quién,
quién, quién? en sombra, en sangre, quién?
en destello, quién,

INVOCATION

To begin, pause over the pure
and cleft rose, pause over the source
of sky and air and earth, the will of a song
with explosions, the desire
of an immense song, of a metal that will gather
war and naked blood.

                    Spain, water glass, not diadem,
but yes crushed stone, militant tenderness
of wheat, hide and burning animal.

Tomorrow, today, in your steps
a silence, an astonishment of hopes
like a major air: a light, a moon,
a worn-out moon, a moon from hand to hand,
from bell to bell!

                  Natal mother, fist
of hardened oats,

              dry
and bloody planet of heroes!
Who? by roads, who,
who, who? in shadows, in blood, who?
in a flash, who,

BOMBARDEO

quién? Cae
ceniza cae,
hierro
y piedra y muerte y llanto y llamas,
quién, quién, madre mía, quién, adónde?

MALDICIÓN

Patria surcada, juro que en tus cenizas
nacerás como flor de agua perpetua,
juro que de tu boca de sed saldrán al aire
los pétalos del pan, la derramada
espiga inaugurada. Malditos sean,
malditos, malditos los que con hacha y serpiente
llegaron a tu arena terrenal, malditos los
que esperaron este día para abrir la puerta
de la mansión al moro y al bandido:
Qué habéis logrado? Traed, traed la lámpara,
ved el suelo empapado, ved el huesito negro
comido por las llamas, la vestidura
de España fusilada.

ESPAÑA POBRE POR CULPA DE LOS RICOS

Malditos los que un día
no miraron, malditos ciegos malditos,
los que no adelantaron a la solemne patria
el pan sino las lágrimas, malditos
uniformes manchados y sotanas
de agrios, hediondos perros de cueva y sepultura.
La pobreza era por España

BOMBARDMENT

who? Ashes
fall, fall,
iron
and stone and death and weeping and flames,
who, who, mother, who, where?

CURSE

Furrowed motherland, I swear that in your ashes
you will be born like a flower of eternal water,
I swear that from your mouth of thirst will come to the air
the petals of bread, the spilt
inaugurated flower. Cursed,
cursed, cursed be those who with ax and serpent
came to your earthly arena, cursed those
who waited for this day to open the door
of the dwelling to the Moor and the bandit:
What have you achieved? Bring, bring the lamp,
see the soaked earth, see the blackened little bone
eaten by the flames, the garment
of murdered Spain.

SPAIN POOR THROUGH THE FAULT OF THE RICH

Cursed be those who one day
did not look, cursed cursed blind,
those who offered the solemn fatherland
not bread but tears, cursed
sullied uniforms and cassocks
of sour, stinking dogs of cave and grave.
Poverty was throughout Spain

como caballos llenos de humo,
como piedras caídas del
manantial de la desventura,
tierras cereales sin
abrir, bodegas secretas
de azul y estaño, ovarios, puertas, arcos
cerrados, profundidades
que querían parir, todo estaba guardado
por triangulares guardias con escopeta,
por curas de color de triste rata,
por lacayos del rey de inmenso culo.
España dura, país manzanar y pino,
te prohibían tus vagos señores:
A no sembrar, a no parir las minas,
a no montar las vacas, al ensimismamiento
de las tumbas, a visitar cada año
el monumento de Cristóbal el marinero, a relinchar
discursos con macacos venidos de América,
iguales en "posición social" y podredumbre.
No levantéis escuelas, no hagáis crujir la cáscara
terrestre con arados, no llenéis los graneros
de abundancia trigal: rezad, bestias, rezad,
que un dios de culo inmenso como el culo del rey
os espera: "Allí tomaréis sopa, hermanos míos."

LA TRADICIÓN

En las noches de España, por los viejos jardines
la tradición, llena de mocos muertos,
chorreando pus y peste se paseaba
con una cola en bruma, fantasmal y fantástica,
vestida de asma y huecos levitones sangrientos,
y su rostro de ojos profundos detenidos

like horses filled with smoke,
like stones fallen from the
spring of misfortune,
grainlands still
unopened, secret storehouses
of blue and tin, ovaries, doors, closed
arches, depths
that tried to give birth, all was guarded
by triangular guards with guns,
by sad-rat-colored priests,
by lackeys of the huge-rumped king.
Tough Spain, land of apple orchards and pines,
your idle lords ordered you:
Do not sow the land, do not give birth to mines,
do not breed cows, but contemplate
the tombs, visit each year
the monument of Columbus the sailor, neigh
speeches with monkeys come from America,
equal in "social position" and in putrefaction.
Do not build schools, do not break open earth's
crust with plows, do not fill the granaries
with abundance of wheat: pray, beasts, pray,
for a god with a rump as huge as the king's rump
awaits you: "There you will have soup, my brethren."

TRADITION

In the nights of Spain, through the old gardens,
tradition, covered with dead snot,
spouting pus and pestilence, strolled
with its tail in the fog, ghostly and fantastic,
dressed in asthma and bloody hollow frock coats,
and its face with sunken staring eyes

eran verdes babosas comiendo tumba,
y su boca sin muelas mordía cada noche
la espiga sin nacer, el mineral secreto,
y pasaba con su corona de cardos verdes
sembrando vagos huesos de difunto y puñales.

MADRID (1936)

Madrid sola y solemne, julio te sorprendió con tu alegría
de panal pobre: clara era tu calle,
claro era tu sueño.
                  Un hipo negro
de generales, una ola
de sotanas rabiosas
rompió entre tus rodillas
sus cenegales aguas, sus ríos de gargajo.

Con los ojos heridos todavía de sueño,
con escopeta y piedras, Madrid, recién herida,
te defendiste. Corrías
por las calles
dejando estelas de tu santa sangre,
reuniendo y llamando con una voz de océano,
con un rostro cambiado para siempre
por la luz de la sangre, como una vengadora
montaña, como una silbante
estrella de cuchillos.

Cuando en los tenebrosos cuarteles, cuando en las sacristías
de la traición entró tu espada ardiendo,
no hubo sino silencio de amanecer, no hubo
sino tu paso de banderas,
y una honorable gota de sangre en tu sonrisa.

was green slugs eating graves,
and its toothless mouth each night bit
the unborn flower, the secret mineral,
and it passed with its crown of green thistles
sowing vague deadmen's bones and daggers.

MADRID (1936)

Madrid, alone and solemn, July surprised you with your joy
of humble honeycomb: bright was your street,
bright was your dream.
                    A black vomit
of generals, a wave
of rabid cassocks
poured between your knees
their swampy waters, their rivers of spittle.

With eyes still wounded by sleep,
with guns and stones, Madrid, newly wounded,
you defended yourself. You ran
though the streets
leaving trails of your holy blood,
rallying and calling with an oceanic voice,
with a face changed forever
by the light of blood, like an avenging
mountain, like a whistling
star of knives.

When into the dark barracks, when into the sacristies
of treason your burning sword entered,
there was only silence of dawn, there was
only your passage of flags,
and an honorable drop of blood in your smile.

Preguntaréis: Y dónde están las lilas?
Y la metafísica cubierta de amapolas?
Y la lluvia que a menudo golpeaba
sus palabras llenándolas
de agujeros y pájaros?

Os voy a contar todo lo que me pasa.

Yo vivía en un barrio
de Madrid, con campanas,
con relojes. con árboles.

Desde allí se veía
el rostro seco de Castilla
como un océano de cuero.
                          Mi casa era llamada
la casa de las flores, porque por todas partes
estallaban geranios: era
una bella casa
con perros y chiquillos.
                         Raúl, te acuerdas?
Te acuerdas, Rafael?
                    Federico, te acuerdas
debajo de la tierra,
te acuerdas de mi casa con balcones en donde
la luz de Junio ahogaba flores en tu boca?
                          Hermano, hermano!

Todo
era grandes voces, sal de mercaderías,
aglomeraciones de pan palpitante,

I Explain a Few Things

You will ask: And where are the lilacs?
And the metaphysical blanket of poppies?
And the rain that often struck
your words filling them
with holes and birds?

I am going to tell you all that is happening to me.

I lived in a quarter
of Madrid, with bells,
with clocks, with trees.

From there one could see
the lean face of Spain
like an ocean of leather.
                            My house was called
the house of flowers, because it was bursting
everywhere with geraniums: it was
a fine house
with dogs and children.
                            Raúl, do you remember?
Do you remember, Rafael?
                            Federico,* do you remember
under the ground,
do you remember my house with balconies where
June light smothered flowers in your mouth?
                                            Brother, brother!

Everything
was great shouting, salty goods,
heaps of throbbing bread,

*Federico was García Lorca.—D.D.W.

mercados de mi barrio de Argüelles con su estatua
como un tintero pálido entre las merluzas:
el aceite llegaba a las cucharas,
un profundo latido
de pies y manos llenaba las calles,
metros, litros, esencia
aguda de la vida,
                         pescados hacinados,
contextura de techos con sol frío en el cual
la flecha se fatiga,
delirante marfil fino de las patatas,
tomates repetidos hasta el mar.

Y una mañana todo estaba ardiendo
y una mañana las hogueras
salían de la tierra
devorando seres,
y desde entonces fuego,
pólvora desde entonces,
y desde entonces sangre.

Bandidos con aviones y con moros,
bandidos con sortijas y duquesas,
bandidos con frailes negros bendiciendo
venían por el cielo a matar niños,
y por las calles la sangre de los niños
corría simplemente, como sangre de niños.

Chacales que el chacal rechazaría,
piedras que el cardo seco mordería escupiendo,
víboras que las víboras odiaran!

Frente a vosotros he visto la sangre
de España levantarse

markets of my Argüelles quarter with its statue
like a pale inkwell among the haddock:
the olive oil reached the ladles,
a deep throbbing
of feet and hands filled the streets,
meters, liters, sharp
essence of life,
                fish piled up,
pattern of roofs with cold sun on which
the vane grows weary,
frenzied fine ivory of the potatoes,
tomatoes stretching to the sea.

And one morning all was aflame
and one morning the fires
came out of the earth
devouring people,
and from then on fire,
gunpowder from then on,
and from then on blood.

Bandits with airplanes and with Moors,
bandits with rings and duchesses,
bandits with black-robed friars blessing
came through the air to kill children,
and through the streets the blood of the children
ran simply, like children's blood.

Jackals that the jackal would spurn,
stones that the dry thistle would bite spitting,
vipers that vipers would abhor!

Facing you I have seen the blood
of Spain rise up

para ahogaros en una sola ola
de orgullo y de cuchillos!

Generales
traidores:
mirad mi casa muerta,
mirad España rota:
pero de cada casa muerta sale metal ardiendo
en vez de flores,
pero de cada hueco de España
sale España,
pero de cada niño muerto sale un fusil con ojos,
pero de cada crimen nacen balas
que os hallarán un día el sitio
del corazón.

Preguntaréis por qué su poesía
no nos habla del sueño, de las hojas,
de los grandes volcanes de su país natal?

Venid a ver la sangre por las calles,
venid a ver
la sangre por las calles,
venid a ver la sangre
por las calles!

CANTO A LAS MADRES DE LOS MILICIANOS MUERTOS

No han muerto! Están en medio
de la pólvora,
de pie, como mechas ardiendo.
Sus sombras puras se han unido
en la pradera de color de cobre
como una cortina de viento blindado,

to drown you in a single wave
of pride and knives!

Treacherous
generals:
look at my dead house,
look at broken Spain:
but from each dead house comes burning metal
instead of flowers,
but from each hollow of Spain
Spain comes forth,
but from each dead child comes a gun with eyes,
but from each crime are born bullets
that will one day seek out in you
where the heart lies.

You will ask: why does your poetry
not speak to us of sleep, of the leaves,
of the great volcanoes of your native land?

Come and see the blood in the streets,
come and see
the blood in the streets,
come and see the blood
in the streets!

SONG FOR THE MOTHERS OF SLAIN MILITIAMEN

They have not died! They are in the midst
of the gunpowder,
standing, like burning wicks.
Their pure shadows have gathered
in the copper-colored meadowland
like a curtain of armored wind,

como una barrera de color de furia,
como el mismo invisible pecho del cielo.

Madres! Ellos están de pie en el trigo,
altos como el profundo mediodía,
dominando las grandes llanuras!
Son una campanada de voz negra
que a través de los cuerpos de acero asesinado
repica la victoria.
                  Hermanas como el polvo
caído, corazones
quebrantados,
tened fe en vuestros muertos!
No sólo son raíces
bajo las piedras teñidas de sangre,
no sólo sus pobres huesos derribados
definitivamente trabajan en la tierra,
sino que aún sus bocas muerden pólvora seca
y atacan como océanos de hierro, y aún
sus puños levantados contradicen la muerte.

Porque de tantos cuerpos una vida invisible
se levanta. Madres, banderas, hijos!
Un solo cuerpo vivo como la vida:
un rostro de ojos rotos vigila las tinieblas
con una espada llena de esperanzas terrestres!

Dejad
vuestros mantos de luto, juntad todas
vuestras lágrimas hasta hacerlas metales:
que allí golpeamos de día y de noche,
allí pateamos de día y de noche,
allí escupimos de día y de noche
hasta que caigan las puertas del odio!

like a barricade the color of fury,
like the invisible heart of heaven itself.

Mothers! They are standing in the wheat,
tall as the depth of noon,
dominating the great plains!
They are a black-voiced bell stroke
that across the bodies murdered by steel
is ringing out victory.
                              Sisters like the fallen
dust, shattered
hearts,
have faith in your dead!
They are not only roots
beneath the bloodstained stones,
not only do their poor demolished bones
definitively till the soil,
but their mouths still bite dry powder
and attack like iron oceans, and still
their upraised fists deny death.

Because from so many bodies an invisible life
rises up. Mothers, banners, sons!
A single body as alive as life:
a face of broken eyes keeps vigil in the darkness
with a sword filled with earthly hopes!

Put aside
your mantles of mourning, join all
your tears until you make them metal:
for there we strike by day and by night,
there we kick by day and by night,
there we spit by day and by night
until the doors of hatred fall!

Yo no me olvido de vuestras desgracias, conozco
vuestros hijos,
y si estoy orgulloso de sus muertes,
estoy también orgulloso de sus vidas.
                                        Sus risas
relampagueaban en los sordos talleres,
sus pasos en el Metro
sonaban a mi lado cada día, y junto
a las naranjas de Levante, a las redes del Sur, junto
a la tinta de las imprentas, sobre el cemento
        de las arquitecturas
he visto llamear sus corazones de fuego y energías.

Y como en vuestros corazones, madres,
hay en mi corazón tanto luto y tanta muerte
que parece una selva
mojada por la sangre que mató sus sonrisas,
y entran en él las rabiosas nieblas del desvelo
con la desgarradora soledad de los días.

Pero
más que la maldición a las hienas sedientas, al
        estertor bestial,
que aúlla desde el África sus patentes inmundas,
más que la cólera, más que el desprecio, más que el llanto,
madres atravesadas por la angustia y la muerte,
mirad el corazón del noble día que nace,
y sabed que vuestros muertos sonríen desde la tierra
levantando los puños sobre el trigo.

I do not forget your misfortunes, I know
your sons,
and if I am proud of their deaths,
I am also proud of their lives.

                              Their laughter
flashed in the silent workshops,
their steps in the subway
sounded at my side each day, and next
to the oranges from the Levant, to the nets from the South, next
to the ink from the printing presses, over the cement
    of the architecture
I have seen their hearts flame with fire and energy.

And just as in your hearts, mothers,
there is in my heart so much mourning and so much death
that it is like a forest
drenched by the blood that killed their smiles,
and into it enter the rabid mists of vigilance
with the rending loneliness of the days.

But
more than curses for the thirsty hyenas, the bestial
    death rattle,
that howls from Africa its filthy privileges,
more than anger, more than scorn, more than weeping,
mothers pierced by anguish and death,
look at the heart of the noble day that is born,
and know that your dead ones smile from the earth
raising their fists above the wheat.

Era España tirante y seca, diurno
tambor de son opaco,
llanura y nido de águilas, silencio
de azotada intemperie.

Cómo, hasta el llanto, hasta el alma
amo tu duro suelo, tu pan pobre,
tu pueblo pobre, cómo hasta el hondo sitio
de mi ser hay la flor perdida de tus aldeas
arrugadas, inmóviles de tiempo,
y tus campiñas minerales
extendidas en luna y en edad
y devoradas por un dios vacío.

Todas tus estructuras, tu animal
aislamiento junto a tu inteligencia
rodeada por las piedras abstractas del silencio,
tu áspero vino, tu suave
vino, tus violentas
y delicadas viñas.

Piedra solar, pura entre las regiones
del mundo, España recorrida
por sangres y metales, azul y victoriosa,
proletaria de pétalos y balas, única
viva y soñolienta y sonora.

Huélamo, Carrascosa,
Alpedrete, Buitrago,
Palencia, Arganda, Galve,
Galapagar, Villalba.

WHAT SPAIN WAS LIKE

Spain was tense and lean, a daily
drum of opaque sound,
plainland and eagle's nest, silence
of scourged inclemency.

How, even to weeping, even to the soul,
I love your hard earth, your humble bread,
your humble people, how even to the deep seat
of my existence there is the lost flower of your wrinkled
villages, motionless in time,
and your mineral countrysides
extended in moon and age
and devoured by an empty god.

All your structures, your animal
isolation next to your intelligence
surrounded by the abstract stones of silence,
your bitter wine, your smooth
wine, your violent
and delicate vineyards.

Ancestral stone, pure among the regions
of the world, Spain crossed
by bloods and metals, blue and victorious,
proletarian of petals and bullets, uniquely
alive and somnolent and resounding.

Huélamo, Carrascosa,*
Alpedrete, Buitrago,
Palencia, Arganda, Galve,
Galapagar, Villalba.

*These are names of Spanish towns and villages.—D.D.W.

Peñarrubia, Cedrillas,
Alcocer, Tamurejo,
Aguadulce, Pedrera,
Fuente Palmera, Colmenar, Sepúlveda.

Carcabuey, Fuencaliente,
Linares, Solana del Pino,
Carcelén, Alatox,
Mahora, Valdeganda.

Yeste, Riopar, Segorbe,
Orihuela, Montalbo,
Alcaraz, Caravaca,
Almendralejo, Castejón de Monegros.

Palma del Río, Peralta,
Granadella, Quintana
de la Serena, Atienza, Barahona,
Navalmoral, Oropesa.

Alborea, Monóvar,
Almansa, San Benito,
Moratalla, Montesa,
Torre Baja, Aldemuz.

Cevico Navero, Cevico de la Torre,
Albalate de las Nogueras,
Jabaloyas, Teruel,
Camporrobles, la Alberca.

Pozo Amargo, Candeleda,
Pedroñeras, Campillo de Altobuey,
Loranca de Tajuña, Puebla de la Mujer Muerta,
Torre la Cárcel, Játiva, Alcoy.

Peñarrubia, Cedrillas,
Alcocer, Tamurejo,
Aguadulce, Pedrera,
Fuente Palmera, Colmenar, Sepúlveda.

Carcabuey, Fuencaliente,
Linares, Solana del Pino,
Carcelén, Alatox,
Mahora, Valdeganda.

Yeste, Riopar, Segorbe,
Orihuela, Montalbo,
Alcaraz, Caravaca,
Almendralejo, Castejón de Monegros.

Palma del Río, Peralta,
Granadella, Quintana
de la Serena, Atienza, Barahona,
Navalmoral, Oropesa.

Alborea, Monóvar,
Almansa, San Benito,
Moratalla, Montesa,
Torre Baja, Aldemuz.

Cevico Navero, Cevico de la Torre,
Albalate de las Nogueras,
Jabaloyas, Teruel,
Camporrobles, la Alberca.

Pozo Amargo, Candeleda,
Pedroñeras, Campillo de Altobuey,
Loranca de Tajuña, Puebla de la Mujer Muerta,
Torre la Cárcel, Játiva, Alcoy.

Pueblo de Obando, Villar del Rey,
Beloraga, Brihuega,
Cetina, Villacañas, Palomas,
Navalcán, Henarejos, Albatana.

Torredonjimeno, Trasparga,
Agramón, Crevillente,
Poveda de la Sierra, Pedernoso,
Alcolea de Cinca, Matallanos.

Ventosa del Rio, Alba de Tormes,
Horcajo Medianero, Piedrahita,
Minglanilla, Navamorcuende, Navalperal,
Navalcarnero, Navalmorales, Jorquera.

Argora, Torremocha, Argecilla,
Ojos Negros, Salvacañete, Utiel,
Laguna Seca, Cañamares, Salorino,
Aldea Quemada, Pesquera de Duero.

Fuenteovejuna, Alpedrete,
Torrejón, Benaguacil,
Valverde de Júcar, Vallanca,
Hiendelaencina, Robledo de Chavela.

Miñogalindo, Ossa de Montiel,
Méntrida, Valdepeñas, Titaguas,
Almodóvar, Gestaldar, Valdemoro,
Almoradiel, Orgaz.

Pueblo de Obando, Villar del Rey,
Beloraga, Brihuega,
Cetina, Villacañas, Palomas,
Navalcán, Henarejos, Albatana.

Torredonjimeno, Trasparga,
Agramón, Crevillente,
Poveda de la Sierra, Pedernoso,
Alcolea de Cinca, Matallanos.

Ventosa del Rio, Alba de Tormes,
Horcajo Medianero, Piedrahita,
Minglanilla, Navamorcuende, Navalperal,
Navalcarnero, Navalmorales, Jorquera.

Argora, Torremocha, Argecilla,
Ojos Negros, Salvacañete, Utiel,
Laguna Seca, Cañamares, Salorino,
Aldea Quemada, Pesquera de Duero.

Fuenteovejuna, Alpedrete,
Torrejón, Benaguacil,
Valverde de Júcar, Vallanca,
Hiendelaencina, Robledo de Chavela.

Miñogalindo, Ossa de Montiel,
Méntrida, Valdepeñas, Titaguas,
Almodóvar, Gestaldar, Valdemoro,
Almoradiel, Orgaz.

Una mañana de un mes frío,
de un mes agonizante, manchado por el lodo y por el humo,
un mes sin rodillas, un triste mes de sitio y desventura,
cuando a través de los cristales mojados de mi casa
    se oían los chacales africanos
aullar con los rifles y los dientes llenos de sangre, entonces,
cuando no teníamos más esperanza que un sueño de pólvora,
    cuando ya creíamos
que el mundo estaba lleno sólo de monstruos devoradores
    y de furias,
entonces, quebrando la escarcha del mes de frío de Madrid,
    en la niebla
del alba
he visto con estos ojos que tengo, con este corazón
    que mira,
he visto llegar a los claros, a los dominadores combatientes
de la delgada y dura y madura y ardiente brigada de piedra.

Era el acongojado tiempo en que las mujeres
llevaban una ausencia como un carbón terrible,
y la muerte española, más ácida y aguda que otras muertes,
llenaba los campos hasta entonces honrados por el trigo.

Por las calles la sangre rota del hombre se juntaba
con el agua que sale del corazón destruido de las casas:
los huesos de los niños deshechos, el desgarrador
enlutado silencio de las madres, los ojos
cerrados para siempre de los indefensos,
eran como la tristeza y la pérdida, eran como un jardín escupido,
eran la fe y la flor asesinadas para siempre.

Camaradas,
entonces

Arrival in Madrid of the International Brigade

One morning in a cold month,
an agonizing month, stained by mud and smoke,
a month without knees, a sad month of siege and misfortune,
when through the wet windows of my house
    the African jackals could be heard
howling with rifles and teeth covered with blood, then,
when we had no more hope than a dream of powder,
    when we already thought
that the world was filled only with devouring monsters
    and furies,
then, breaking the frost of the cold Madrid month,
    in the fog
of the dawn
I saw with these eyes that I have, with this heart
    that looks,
I saw arrive the clear, the masterful fighters
of the thin and hard and mellow and ardent stone brigade.

It was the anguished time when women
wore absence like a frightful coal,
and Spanish death, more acrid and sharper than other deaths,
filled fields up to then honored by wheat.

Through the streets the broken blood of man joined
the water that emerges from the ruined hearts of homes:
the bones of the shattered children, the heartrending
black-clad silence of the mothers, the eyes
forever shut of the defenseless,
were like sadness and loss, were like a spit-upon garden,
were faith and flower forever murdered.

Comrades,
then

os he visto,
y mis ojos están hasta ahora llenos de orgullo
porque os vi a través de la mañana de niebla llegar
     a la frente pura de Castilla
silenciosos y firmes
como campanas antes del alba,
llenos de solemnidad y de ojos azules venir de lejos
     y lejos,
venir de vuestros rincones, de vuestras patrias perdidas,
     de vuestros sueños
llenos de dulzura quemada y de fusiles
a defender la ciudad española en que la libertad acorralada
pudo caer y morir mordida por las bestias.

Hermanos, que desde ahora
vuestra pureza y vuestra fuerza, vuestra historia solemne
sea conocida del niño y del varón, de la mujer y del viejo,
llegue a todos los seres sin esperanza, baje a las minas
     corroídas por el aire sulfúrico,
suba a las escaleras inhumanas del esclavo,
que todas las estrellas, que todas las espigas de Castilla
     y del mundo
escriban vuestro nombre y vuestra áspera lucha
y vuestra victoria fuerte y terrestre como una encina roja.
Porque habéis hecho renacer con vuestro sacrificio
la fe perdida, el alma ausente, la confianza en la tierra,
y por vuestra abundancia, por vuestra nobleza, por
     vuestros muertos,
como por un valle de duras rocas de sangre,
pasa un inmenso río con palomas de acero y de esperanza.

I saw you,
and my eyes are even now filled with pride
because through the misty morning I saw you reach
    the pure brow of Castile
silent and firm
like bells before dawn,
filled with solemnity and blue-eyed, come from far,
    far away,
come from your corners, from your lost fatherlands,
    from your dreams,
covered with burning gentleness and guns
to defend the Spanish city in which besieged liberty
could fall and die bitten by the beasts.

Brothers, from now on
let your pureness and your strength, your solemn story
be known by children and by men, by women and by old men,
let it reach all men without hope, let it go down to the mines
    corroded by sulphuric air,
let it mount the inhuman stairways of the slave,
let all the stars, let all the flowers of Castile
    and of the world
write your name and your bitter struggle
and your victory strong and earthen as a red oak.
Because you have revived with your sacrifice
lost faith, absent heart, trust in the earth,
and through your abundance, through your nobility, through
    your dead,
as if through a valley of harsh bloody rocks,
flows an immense river with doves of steel and of hope.

Entre la tierra y el platino ahogado
de olivares y muertos españoles,
Jarama, puñal puro, has resistido
　　　　la ola de los crueles.

Allí desde Madrid llegaron hombres
de corazón dorado por la pólvora
como un pan de ceniza y resistencia,
　　　　allí llegaron.

Jarama, estabas entre hierro y humo
como una rama de cristal caído,
como una larga línea de medallas
　　　　para los victoriosos.

Ni socavones de substancia ardiendo,
ni coléricos vuelos explosivos,
ni artillería de tiniebla turbia
　　　　dominaron tus aguas.

Aguas tuyas bebieron los sedientos
de sangre, agua bebieron boca arriba:
agua española y tierra de olivares
　　　　los llenaron de olvido.

Por un segundo de agua y tiempo el cauce
de la sangre de moros y traidores
palpitaba en tu luz como los peces
　　　　de un manantial amargo.

BATTLE OF THE JARAMA RIVER*

Between the earth and the drowned platinum
of olive orchards and Spanish dead,
Jarama, pure dagger, you have resisted
       the wave of the cruel.

There, from Madrid, came men
with hearts made golden by gunpowder,
like a loaf of ashes and resistance,
       there they came.

Jarama, you were between iron and smoke
like a branch of fallen crystal,
like a long line of medals
       for the victorious.

Neither caverns of burning substance,
nor angry explosive flights,
nor artillery of turbid darkness
       controlled your waters.

The bloodthirsty drank
your waters, face up they drank water:
Spanish water and olive fields
       filled them with oblivion.

For a second of water and time the river bed
of the blood of Moors and traitors
throbbed in your light like the fish
       of a bitter fountain.

*In February 1937 the Republican army, aided by the International Brigade, repulsed a Nationalist attack at the Jarama River near Madrid and thereby kept open the road to Valencia and Catalonia.—D.D.W.

La áspera harina de tu pueblo estaba
toda erizada de metal y huesos,
formidable y trigal como la noble
        tierra que defendían.

Jarama, para hablar de tus regiones
de esplendor y dominio, no es mi boca
suficiente, y es pálida mi mano:
        allí quedan tus muertos.

Allí quedan tu cielo doloroso,
tu paz de piedra, tu estelar corriente,
y los eternos ojos de tu pueblo
        vigilan tus orillas.

ALMERÍA

Un plato para el obispo, un plato triturado y amargo,
un plato con restos de hierro, con cenizas, con lágrimas,
un plato sumergido, con sollozos y paredes caídas,
un plato para el obispo, un plato de sangre de Almería.

Un plato para el banquero, un plato con mejillas
de niños del Sur feliz, un plato
con detonaciones, con aguas locas y ruinas y espanto,
un plato con ejes partidos y cabezas pisadas,
un plato negro, un plato de sangre de Almería.

Cada mañana, cada mañana turbia de vuestra vida
lo tendréis humeante y ardiente en vuestra mesa:

The bitter wheat of your people was
all bristling with metal and bones,
formidable and germinal like the noble
        land that they defended.

Jarama, to speak of your regions
of splendor and dominion, my mouth is not
adequate, and my hand is pale:
        there rest your dead.

There rest your mournful sky,
your flinty peace, your starry stream,
and the eternal eyes of your people
        watch over your shores.

ALMERÍA*

A bowl for the bishop, a crushed and bitter bowl,
a bowl with remnants of iron, with ashes, with tears,
a sunken bowl, with sobs and fallen walls,
a bowl for the bishop, a bowl of Almería blood.

A bowl for the banker, a bowl with cheeks
of children from the happy South, a bowl
with explosions, with wild waters and ruins and fright,
a bowl with split axles and trampled heads,
a black bowl, a bowl of Almería blood.

Each morning, each turbid morning of your lives
you will have it steaming and burning at your tables:

*In February 1937 hundreds of Republican civilians, fleeing from Málaga toward Almería, were overtaken by Nationalist planes and tanks. The men and boys were executed in the presence of their wives and mothers.—D.D.W.

para no verlo, para no digerirlo tantas veces:
lo apartaréis un poco entre el pan y las uvas,
a este plato de sangre silenciosa
que estará allí cada mañana, cada
mañana.

Un plato para el coronel y la esposa del coronel,
en una fiesta de la guarnición, en cada fiesta,
sobre los juramentos y los escupos, con la luz de vino
    de la madrugada
para que lo veáis temblando y frío sobre el mundo.

Sí, un plato para todos vosotros, ricos de aquí y de allá,
embajadores, ministros, comensales atroces,
señoras de confortable té y asiento:
un plato destrozado, desbordado, sucio de sangre pobre,
para cada mañana, para cada semana, para siempre jamás,
un plato de sangre de Almería, ante vosotros, siempre.

TIERRAS OFENDIDAS

Regiones sumergidas
en el interminable martirio, por el inacabable
silencio, pulsos
de abeja y roca exterminada,
tierras que en vez de trigo y trébol
traéis señal de sangre seca y crimen:
caudalosa Galicia, pura como la lluvia,
salada para siempre por las lágrimas:
Extremadura, en cuya orilla augusta
de cielo y aluminio, negro como agujero
de bala, traicionado y herido y destrozado,

so as not to see it, not to digest it so many times:
you will push it aside a bit between the bread and the grapes,
this bowl of silent blood
that will be there each morning, each
morning.

A bowl for the Colonel and the Colonel's wife
at a garrison party, at each party,
above the oaths and the spittle, with the wine light of early
morning
so that you may see it trembling and cold upon the world.

Yes, a bowl for all of you, richmen here and there,
monstrous ambassadors, ministers, table companions,
ladies with cozy tea parties and chairs:
a bowl shattered, overflowing, dirty with the blood of the poor,
for each morning, for each week, forever and ever,
a bowl of Almería blood, facing you, forever.

OFFENDED LANDS

Regions submerged
in interminable martyrdom, through the unending
silence, pulses
of bee and exterminated rock,
you lands that instead of wheat and clover
bring signs of dried blood and crime:
abundant Galicia, pure as rain,
made salty forever by tears:
Extremadura, on whose august shore
of sky and aluminum, black as a bullet
hole, betrayed and wounded and shattered:

Badajoz sin memoria, entre sus hijos muertos
yace mirando un cielo que recuerda:
Málaga arada por la muerte
y perseguida entre los precipicios
hasta que las enloquecidas madres
azotaban la piedra con sus recién nacidos.
Furor, vuelo de luto
y muerte y cólera,
hasta que ya las lágrimas y el duelo reunidos,
hasta que las palabras y el desmayo y la ira
no son sino un montón de huesos en un camino
y una piedra enterrada por el polvo.

Es tanto, tanta
tumba, tanto martirio, tanto
galope de bestias en la estrella!
Nada, ni la victoria
borrará el agujero terrible de la sangre:
nada, ni el mar, ni el paso
de arena y tiempo, ni el geranio ardiendo
sobre la sepultura.

SANJURJO EN LOS INFIERNOS

Amarrado, humeante, acordelado
a su traidor avión, a sus traiciones,
se quema el traidor traicionado.

Como fósforo queman sus riñones
y su siniestra boca de soldado
traidor se derrite en maldiciones,

Badajoz without memory, among her dead sons
she lies watching a sky that remembers:
Málaga plowed by death
and pursued among the cliffs
until the maddened mothers
beat upon the rock with their newborn sons.
Furor, flight of mourning
and death and anger,
until the tears and grief now gathered,
until the words and the fainting and the anger
are only a pile of bones in a road
and a stone buried by the dust.

It is so much, so many
tombs, so much martyrdom, so much
galloping of beasts in the star!
Nothing, not even victory
will erase the terrible hollow of the blood:
nothing, neither the sea, nor the passage
of sand and time, nor the geranium flaming
upon the grave.

SANJURJO* IN HELL

Tied up, reeking, roped
to his betraying airplane, to his betrayals,
the betrayed betrayer burns.

Like phosphorus his kidneys burn
and his sinister betraying soldier's
mouth melts in curses,

*General José Sanjurjo, 1872–1936, an early and leading plotter against the Republic.—D.D.W.

37

por las eternas llamas piloteado,
conducido y quemado por aviones,
de traición en traición quemado.

MOLA EN LOS INFIERNOS

Es arrastrado el turbio mulo Mola
de precipicio en precipicio eterno
y como va el naufragio de ola en ola,
desbaratado por azufre y cuerno,
cocido en cal y hiel y disimulo,
de antemano esperado en el infierno,
va el infernal mulato, el Mola mulo
definitivamente turbio y tierno,
con llamas en la cola y en el culo.

EL GENERAL FRANCO EN LOS INFIERNOS

*Desventurado, ni el fuego ni el vinagre caliente
en un nido de brujas volcánicas, ni el hielo devorante,
ni la tortuga pútrida que ladrando y llorando con
   voz de mujer muerta te escarbe la barriga
buscando una sortija nupcial y un juguete de niño degollado,
serán para ti nada sino una puerta oscura,
arrasada.*

    En efecto.
*De infierno a infierno, qué hay? En el aullido
de tus legiones, en la santa leche
de las madres de España, en la leche y los senos pisoteados*

piloted through the eternal flames,
guided and burnt by airplanes,
burnt from betrayal to betrayal.

MOLA* IN HELL

The turbid Mola mule is dragged
from cliff to eternal cliff
and as the shipwrecked man goes from wave to wave,
destroyed by brimstone and horn,
boiled in lime and gall and deceit,
already expected in hell,
the infernal mulatto goes, the Mola mule
definitively turbid and tender,
with flames on his tail and his rump.

GENERAL FRANCO IN HELL

*Evil one, neither fire nor hot vinegar
in a nest of volcanic witches, nor devouring ice,
nor the putrid turtle that barking and weeping with the
    voice of a dead woman scratches your belly
seeking a wedding ring and the toy of a slaughtered child,
will be for you anything but a dark demolished
door.*

*   Indeed.
From one hell to another, what difference? In the howling
of your legions, in the holy milk
of the mothers of Spain, in the milk and the bosoms trampled*

*General Emilio Mola, 1887–1937, commander of the Nationalist northern
army, killed in an airplane accident.—D.D.W.

39

por los caminos, hay una aldea más, un silencio más, una
  puerta rota.

        Aquí estás. Triste párpado, estiércol
de siniestras gallinas de sepulcro, pesado esputo, cifra
de traición que la sangre no borra. Quién, quién eres,
oh miserable hoja de sal, oh perro de la tierra,
oh mal nacida palidez de sombra.

        Retrocede la llama sin ceniza,
la sed salina del infierno, los círculos
del dolor palidecen.

        Maldito, que sólo lo humano
te persiga, que dentro del absoluto fuego de las cosas,
no te consumas, que no te pierdas
en la escala del tiempo, y que no te taladre el vidrio ardiendo
ni la feroz espuma.
                Solo, solo, para las lágrimas
todas reunidas, para una eternidad de manos muertas
y ojos podridos, solo en una cueva
de tu infierno, comiendo silenciosa pus y sangre
por una eternidad maldita y sola.
                        No mereces dormir
aunque sea clavados de alfileres los ojos:
  debes estar
despierto, general, despierto enternamente
entre la podredumbre de las recién paridas,
ametralladas en otoño. Todas, todos los tristes niños
  descuartizados,
tiesos, están colgados, esperando en tu infierno
ese día de fiesta fría: tu llegada.
                        Niños negros por la explosión,
trozos rojos de seso, corredores

along the roads, there is one more village, one more silence,
  a broken door.

       Here you are. Wretched eyelid, dung
of sinister sepulchral hens, heavy sputum, figure
of treason that blood will not erase. Who, who are you,
oh miserable leaf of salt, oh dog of the earth,
oh ill-born pallor of shadow.

       The flame retreats without ash,
the salty thirst of hell, the circles
of grief turn pale.

       Cursed one, may only humans
pursue you, within the absolute fire of things may
you not be consumed, not be lost
in the scale of time, may you not be pierced by the burning glass
or the fierce foam.
               Alone, alone, for the tears
all gathered, for an eternity of dead hands
and rotted eyes, alone in a cave
of your hell, eating silent pus and blood
though a cursed and lonely eternity.
                      You do not deserve to sleep
even though it be with your eyes fastened with pins:
  you have to be
awake, General, eternally awake
among the putrefaction of the new mothers,
machine-gunned in the autumn. All and all the sad children
  cut to pieces,
rigid, they hang, awaiting in your hell
that day of cold festivity: your arrival.
                    Children blackened by explosions,
red fragments of brain, corridors filled

de dulces intestinos, te esperan todos, todos, en la
  misma actitud
de atravesar la calle, de patear la pelota,
de tragar una fruta, de sonreír o nacer.

Sonreír. Hay sonrisas
ya demolidas por la sangre
que esperan con dispersos dientes exterminados,
y máscaras de confusa materia, rostros huecos
de pólvora perpetua, y los fantasmas
sin nombre, los oscuros
escondidos, los que nunca salieron
de su cama de escombros. Todos te esperan
para pasar la noche. Llenan los corredores
como algas corrompidas.
                    Son nuestros, fueron nuestra
carne, nuestra salud, nuestra
paz de herrerías, nuestro océano
de aire y pulmones. A través de ellos
las secas tierras florecían. Ahora, más allá de la tierra,
hechos substancia
destruida, materia asesinada, harina muerta,
te esperan en tu infierno.

Como el agudo espanto o el dolor se consumen,
ni espanto ni dolor te aguardan. Solo y
  maldito seas,
solo y despierto seas entre todos los muertos,
y que la sangre caiga en ti como la lluvia,
y que un agonizante río de ojos cortados
te resbale y recorra mirándote sin término.

with gentle intestines, they all await you, all in the
  very posture
of crossing the street, of kicking the ball,
of swallowing a fruit, of smiling, or being born.

Smiling. There are smiles
now demolished by blood
that wait with scattered exterminated teeth,
and masks of muddled matter, hollow faces
of perpetual gunpowder, and the nameless
ghosts, the dark
hidden ones, those who never left
their beds of rubble. They all wait for you
to spend the night. They fill the corridors
like decayed seaweed.
                    They are ours, they were our
flesh, our health, our
bustling peace, our ocean
of air and lungs. Through
them the dry earth flowered. Now, beyond the earth,
turned into destroyed
substance, murdered matter, dead flour,
they await you in your hell.

Since acute terror or sorrow waste away,
neither terror nor sorrow await you. May you be alone
  and accursed,
alone and awake among all the dead,
and let blood fall upon you like rain,
and let a dying river of severed eyes
slide and flow over you staring at you endlessly.

Esto que fue creado y dominado,
esto que fue humedecido, usado, visto,
yace—pobre pañuelo—entre las olas
de tierra y negro azufre.

                Como el botón o el pecho
se levantan al cielo, como la flor que sube
desde el hueso destruido, así las formas
del mundo aparecieron. Oh párpados,
oh columnas, oh escalas.

                Oh profundas materias
agregadas y puras: cuánto hasta ser campanas!
cuánto hasta ser relojes! Aluminio
de azules proporciones, cemento
pegado al sueño de los seres!

                El polvo se congrega,
la goma, el lodo, los objetos crecen
y las paredes se levantan
como parras de oscura piel humana.

                  Allí dentro en blanco, en cobre,
en fuego, en abandono, los papeles crecían,
el llanto abominable, las prescripciones
llevadas en la noche a la farmacia mientras
alguien con fiebre,
la seca sien mental, la puerta
que el hombre ha construido
para no abrir jamás.

                Todo ha ido y caído
brutalmente marchito.

                  Utensilios heridos, telas
nocturnas, espuma sucia, orines justamente
vertidos, mejillas, vidrio, lana,
alcanfor, círculos de hilo y cuero, todo,

SONG ABOUT SOME RUINS

This that was created and tamed,
this that was moistened, used, seen,
lies—poor kerchief—among the waves
of earth and black brimstone.

                              Like bud or breast
they raise themselves to the sky, like the flower that rises
from the destroyed bone, so the shapes
of the world appeared. Oh eyelids,
oh columns, oh ladders.

                              Oh deep substances
annexed and pure: how long until you are bells!
how long until you are clocks! Aluminum
of blue proportions, cement
stuck to human dreams!

                              The dust gathers,
the gum, the mud, the objects grow
and the walls rise up
like arbors of dark human flesh.

                              Inside there in white, in copper,
in fire, in abandonment, the papers grew,
the abominable weeping, the prescriptions
taken at night to the drugstore while
someone with a fever,
the dry temple of the mind, the door
that man has built
never to open it.

                              Everything has gone and fallen
suddenly withered.

                              Wounded tools, nocturnal
cloths, dirty foam, urine just then
spilt, cheeks, glass, wool,
camphor, circles of thread and leather, all,

todo por una rueda vuelto al polvo,
al desorganizado sueño de los metales,
todo el perfume, todo lo fascinado,
todo reunido en nada, todo caído
para no nacer nunca.

          Sed celeste, palomas
con cintura de harina: épocas
de polen y racimo, ved cómo
la madera se destroza
hasta llegar al luto: no hay raíces
para el hombre: todo descansa apenas
sobre un temblor de lluvia.

              Ved cómo se ha podrido
la guitarra en la boca de la fragante novia:
ved cómo las palabras que tanto construyeron
ahora son exterminio: mirad sobre la cal y entre el
    mármol deshecho
la huella—ya con musgos—del sollozo.

LA VICTORIA DE LAS ARMAS DEL PUEBLO

*Mas, como el recuerdo de la tierra, como el pétreo
esplendor del metal y el silencio,
pueblo, patria y avena, es tu victoria.*

*Avanza tu bandera agujereada
como tu pecho sobre las cicatrices
de tiempo y tierra.*

all through a wheel returned to dust,
to the disorganized dream of the metals,
all the perfume, all the fascination,
all united in nothing, all fallen
never to be born.

     Celestial thirst, doves
with a waist of wheat: epochs
of pollen and branch: see how
the wood is shattered
until it reaches mourning: there are no roots
for man: all scarcely rests
upon a tremor of rain.

     See how the guitar
has rotted in the mouth of the fragrant bride:
see how the words that built so much
now are extermination: upon the lime and among the shattered
  marble, look
at the trace—now moss-covered—of the sob.

THE VICTORY OF THE ARMS OF THE PEOPLE

But, like earth's memory, like the stony
splendor of metal and silence,
is your victory, people, fatherland, and grain.

Your riddled banner advances
like your breast above the scars
of time and earth.

Dónde están los mineros, dónde están
los que hacen el cordel, los que maduran
la suela, los que mandan la red?
Dónde están?

Dónde los que cantaban en lo alto
del edificio, escupiendo y jurando
sobre el cemento aéreo?

Dónde están los ferroviarios
voluntariosos y nocturnos?
Dónde está el gremio del abasto?

Con un fusil, con un fusil. Entre los
pardos latidos de la llanura,
mirando sobre los escombros.

Dirigiendo la bala al duro
enemigo como a las espinas,
como a las víboras, así.

De día y noche, en la ceniza
triste del alba, en la virtud
del mediodía calcinado.

TRIUNFO

Solemne es el triunfo del pueblo,
a su paso de gran victoria
la ciega patata y la uva
celeste brillan en la tierra.

THE UNIONS AT THE FRONT

Where are the miners, where are
the rope makers, the leather
curers, those who cast the nets?
Where are they?

Where are those who used to sing at the top
of the building, spitting and swearing
upon the lofty cement?

Where are the railroadmen
dedicated and nocturnal?
Where is the supplier's union?

With a rifle, with a rifle. Among the
dark throbbing of the plainland,
looking out over the debris.

Aiming the bullet at the harsh
enemy as at the thorns,
as at the vipers, that's it.

By day and by night, in the sad
ash of dawn, in the virtue
of the scorched noon.

TRIUMPH

Solemn is the triumph of the people,
at its great victorious passage
the eyeless potato and the heavenly
grape glitter in the earth.

Mordido espacio, tropa restregada
contra los cereales, herraduras
rotas, heladas entre escarcha y piedras,
          áspera luna.

Luna de yegua herida, calcinada,
envuelta en agotadas espinas, amenazante, hundido
metal o hueso, ausencia, paño amargo,
          humo de enterradores.

Detrás del agrio nimbo de nitratos,
de substancia en substancia, de agua en agua,
rápidos como trigo desgranado,
          quemados y comidos.

Casual corteza suavemente suave,
negra ceniza ausente y esparcida,
ahora sólo frío sonoro, abominables
          materiales de lluvia.

Guárdenlo mis rodillas enterrado
más que este fugitivo territorio,
agárrenlo mis párpados hasta nombrar y herir,
guarde mi sangre este sabor de sombra
          para que no haya olvido.

ANTITANQUISTAS

Ramos todos de clásico nácar, aureolas
de mar y cielo, viento de laureles
para vosotros, encinares héroes,

LANDSCAPE AFTER A BATTLE

Bitten space, troop crushed
against the grain, broken
horseshoes, frozen between frost and stones,
      harsh moon.

Moon of a wounded mare, charred,
wrapped in exhausted thorns, menacing, sunken
metal or bone, absence, bitter cloth,
      smoke of gravediggers.

Behind the acrid halo of saltpeter,
from substance to substance, from water to water,
swift as threshed wheat,
      burned and eaten.

Accidental crust softly soft,
black ash absent and scattered,
now only echoing cold, abominable
      materials of rain.

May my knees keep it hidden
more than this fugitive territory,
may my eyelids grasp it until they can name and wound,
may my blood keep this taste of shadow
      so that there will be no forgetting.

ANTITANKERS

Branches all of classic mother-of-pearl, halos
of sea and sky, wind of laurels
for you, oaken heroes,

antitanquistas.
Habéis sido en la nocturna boca
de la guerra
los ángeles del fuego, los temibles,
los hijos puros de la tierra.

Así estabais, sembrados
en los campos, oscuros, como siembra, tendidos
esperando. Y ante el huracanado hierro, en el pecho
    del monstruo
habéis lanzado, no sólo un trozo pálido de explosivo,
sino vuestro profundo corazón humeante,
látigo destructivo y azul como la pólvora.
Os habéis levantado,
finos celestes contra las montañas
de la crueldad, hijos desnudos
de la tierra y la gloria.
                  Vosotros nunca visteis
antes sino la oliva, nunca sino las redes
llenas de escama y plata: vosotros agrupasteis
los instrumentos, la madera, el hierro
de las cosechas y de las construcciones:
en vuestras manos floreció la bella
granada forestal o la cebolla
matutina, y de pronto
estáis aquí cargados con relámpagos
apretando la gloria, estallando
de poderes furiosos,
solos y duros frente a las tinieblas.

La Libertad os recogió en las minas,
y pidió paz para vuestros arados:
la Libertad se levantó llorando
por los caminos, gritó en los corredores

antitankers.
You have been in the night mouth
of war
the angels of fire, the fearsome ones,
the pure sons of the earth.

That's how you were, planted
in the fields, dark, like seeds, lying
waiting. And before the hurricaned iron, at the chest
    of the monster,
you launched not just a pale bit of explosive
but your deep steaming heart,
a lash as destructive and blue as gunpowder.
You rose up,
noble, heavenly against the mountains
of cruelty, naked sons
of earth and glory.
                    Once you saw
only the olive branch, only the nets
filled with scales and silver: you gathered
the instruments, the wood, the iron
of the harvests and the building:
in your hands flourished the beautiful
forest pomegranate or the morning
onion, and suddenly
you are here laden with lightning,
clutching glory, bursting
with furious powers,
alone and harsh facing the darkness.

Liberty sought you out in the mines,
and begged for peace for your ploughs:
Liberty rose weeping
along the roads, shouted in the corridors

de las casas: en las campiñas
su voz pasaba entre naranja y viento
llamando hombres de pecho maduro, y acudisteis,
y aquí estáis, preferidos
hijos de la victoria, muchas veces caídos, muchas veces
borradas vuestras manos, rotos los más ocultos cartílagos,
    calladas
vuestras bocas, machacado
hasta la destrucción vuestro silencio:
pero surgís de pronto, en medio
del torbellino, otra vez, otros, toda
vuestra insondable, vuestra quemadora
raza de corazones y raíces.

MADRID (1937)

En esta hora recuerdo a todo y todos,
fibradamente, hundidamente en
las regiones que—sonido y pluma—
golpeando un poco, existen
más allá de la tierra, pero en la tierra. Hoy
comienza un nuevo invierno.
               No hay en esa ciudad,
en donde está lo que amo,
no hay pan ni luz: un cristal frío cae
sobre secos geranios. De noche sueños negros
abiertos por obuses, como sangrientos bueyes:
nadie en el alba de las fortificaciones,
sino un carro quebrado: ya musgo, ya silencio de edades
en vez de golondrinas en las casas quemadas,
desangradas, vacías, con puertas hacia el cielo:
ya comienza el mercado a abrir sus pobres esmeraldas,
y las naranjas, el pescado,

of the houses: in the countryside
her voice passed between orange and wind
calling for ripe-hearted men, and you came,
and here you are, the chosen
sons of victory, many times fallen, your hands
many times blotted out, broken the most hidden bones,
    your mouths
stilled, pounded
to destruction your silence:
but you surged up suddenly, in the midst
of the whirlwind, again, others, all
your unfathomable, your burning
race of hearts and roots.

MADRID (1937)

At this hour I remember everything and everyone,
vigorously, sunkenly in
the regions that—sound and feather—
striking a little, exist
beyond the earth, but on the earth. Today
a new winter begins.
              There is in that city,
where lies what I love,
there is no bread, no light: a cold windowpane falls
upon dry geraniums. By night black dreams
opened by howitzers, like bloody oxen:
no one in the dawn of the ramparts
but a broken cart: now moss, now silence of ages,
instead of swallows, on the burned houses,
drained of blood, empty, their doors open to the sky:
now the market begins to open its poor emeralds,
and the oranges, the fish,

cada día traídos a través de la sangre,
se ofrecen a las manos de la hermana y la viuda.
Ciudad de luto, socavada, herida,
rota, golpeada, agujereada, llena
de sangre y vidrios rotos, ciudad sin noche, toda
noche y silencio y estampido y héroes,
ahora un nuevo invierno más desnudo y más solo,
ahora sin harina, sin pasos, con tu luna
de soldados.

        A todo, a todos.

                Sol pobre, sangre nuestra
perdida, corazón terrible
sacudido y llorando. Lágrimas como pesadas balas
han caído en tu oscura tierra haciendo sonido
de palomas que caen, mano que cierra
la muerte para siempre, sangre de cada día
y cada noche y cada semana y cada
mes. Sin hablar de vosotros, héroes dormidos
y despiertos, sin hablar de vosotros que hacéis temblar
  el agua
y la tierra con vuestra voluntad insigne,
en esta hora escucho el tiempo en una calle,
alguien me habla, el invierno
llega de nuevo a los hoteles
en que he vivido,
todo es ciudad lo que escucho y distancia
rodeada por el fuego como por una espuma
de víboras, asaltada por una
agua de infierno.

              Hace ya más de un año
que los enmascarados tocan tu humana orilla
y mueren al cantacto de tu eléctrica sangre:
sacos de moros, sacos de traidores,
han rodado a tus pies de piedra: ni el humo ni la muerte
han conquistado tus muros ardiendo.

brought each day across the blood,
offer themselves to the hands of the sister and the widow.
City of mourning, undermined, wounded,
broken, beaten, bullet-riddled, covered
with blood and broken glass, city without night, all
night and silence and explosions and heroes,
now a new winter more naked and more alone,
now without flour, without steps, with your moon
of soldiers.
   Everything, everyone.
        Poor sun, our lost
blood, terrible heart
shaken and mourned. Tears like heavy bullets
have fallen on your dark earth sounding
like falling doves, a hand that death
closes forever, blood of each day
and each night and each week and each
month. Without speaking of you, heroes asleep
and awake, without speaking of you who make the water
 and the earth
tremble with your glorious purpose,
at this hour I listen to the weather on a street,
someone speaks to me, winter
comes again to the hotels
where I have lived,
everything is city that I listen to and distance
surrounded by fire as if by a spume
of vipers assaulted by a
water of hell.
    For more than a year now
the masked ones have been touching your human shore
and dying at the contact of your electric blood:
sacks of Moors, sacks of traitors
have rolled at your feet of stone: neither smoke nor death
have conquered your burning walls.

Entonces,
qué hay, entonces? Sí, son los del exterminio,
son los devoradores: te acechan, ciudad blanca,
el obispo de turbio testuz, los señoritos
fecales y feudales, el general en cuya mano
suenan treinta dineros: están contra tus muros
un cinturón de lluviosas beatas,
un escuadrón de embajadores pútridos
y un triste hipo de perros militares.

Loor a ti, loor en nube, en rayo,
en salud, en espadas,
frente sangrante cuyo hilo de sangre
reverbera en las piedras malheridas,
deslizamiento de dulzura dura,
clara cuna en relámpagos armada,
material ciudadela, aire de sangre
del que nacen abejas.
                    Hoy tú que vives, Juan,
hoy tú que miras, Pedro, concibes, duermes, comes:
hoy en la noche sin luz vigilando sin sueño
   y sin reposo,
solos en el cemento, por la tierra cortada,
desde los enlutados alambres, al Sur, en medio, en
   torno,
sin cielo, sin misterio,
hombres como un collar de cordones defienden
la ciudad rodeada por las llamas: Madrid endurecida
por golpe astral, par conmoción del fuego:
tierra y vigilia en el alto silencio
de la victoria: sacudida
como una rosa rota: rodeada
de laurel infinito!

Then,
what's happening, then? Yes, they are the exterminators,
they are the devourers: they spy on you, white city,
the bishop of turbid scruff, the fecal and feudal
young masters, the general in whose hand
jingle thirty coins: against your walls are
a circle of women, dripping and devout,
a squadron of putrid ambassadors,
and a sad vomit of military dogs.

Praise to you, praise in cloud, in sunray,
in health, in swords,
bleeding front whose thread of blood
echoes on the deeply wounded stones,
a slipping away of harsh sweetness,
bright cradle armed with lightning,
fortress substance, air of blood
from which bees are born.
                    Today you who live, Juan,
today you who watch, Pedro, who conceive, sleep, eat:
today in the lightless night on guard without sleep
   and without rest,
alone on the cement, across the gashed earth,
from the blackened wire, to the South, in the middle, all
   around,
without sky, without mystery,
men like a collar of cordons defend
the city surrounded by flames: Madrid hardened
by an astral blow, by the shock of fire:
earth and vigil in the deep silence
of victory: shaken
like a broken rose, surrounded
by infinite laurel!

Armas del pueblo! Aquí! La amenaza, el asedio
aún derraman la tierra mezclándola de muerte,
áspera de aguijones!
                    Salud, salud,
salud te dicen las madres del mundo,
las escuelas te dicen salud, los viejos carpinteros,
Ejército del Pueblo, te dicen salud, con las espigas,
la leche, las patatas, el limón, el laurel,
todo lo que es de la tierra y de la boca
del hombre.
                    Todo, como un collar
de manos, como una
cintura palpitante, como una obstinación de relámpagos,
todo a ti se prepara, todo hacia ti converge!
                                        Día de hierro,
azul fortificado!
                    Hermanos, adelante,
adelante por las tierras aradas,
adelante en la noche seca y sin sueño, delirante y raída,
adelante entre vides, pisando el color frío de las rocas,
salud, salud, seguid. Más cortantes que la voz del invierno,
más sensibles que el párpado, más seguros que la punta
        del trueno,
puntuales como el rápido diamante, nuevamente marciales,
guerreros según el agua acerada de las tierras del centro,
según la flor y el vino, según el corazón
        espiral de la tierra,
según las raíces de todas las hojas, de todas las mercaderías
        fragantes de la tierra.
Salud, soldados, salud, barbechos rojos,
salud, tréboles duros, salud, pueblos parados

Arms of the people! Here! The threat, the siege
are still wasting the earth, mixing it with death,
earth rough with goading!
                              Your health,
your health say the mothers of the world,
the schools say your health, the old carpenters,
Army of the People, they say health to you with blossoms,
milk, potatoes, lemon, laurel,
everything that belongs to the earth and to the mouth
of man.
              Everything, like a necklace
of hands, like a
throbbing waist, like a persistence of thunderbolts,
everything prepares itself for you, converges on you!
                                        Day of iron,
fortified blue!
                    Brothers, onward,
onward through the ploughed lands,
onward in the dry and sleepless night, delirious and threadbare,
onward among the vines, treading the cold color of the rocks,
good health to you, go on. More cutting than winter's voice,
more sensitive than the eyelid, more unfailing than the tip
      of the thunderbolt,
exact as the swift diamond, warlike anew,
warriors according to the biting waters of the central lands,
according to the flower and the wine, according to the spiral
      heart of the earth,
according to the roots of all the leaves, of all the fragrant
      produce of the earth.
Your health, soldiers, your health, red fallow lands,
health, hard clovers, health, towns stopped

en la luz del relámpago, salud, salud, salud,
adelante, adelante, adelante, adelante,
sobre las minas, sobre los cementerios, frente al abominable
apetito de muerte, frente al erizado
terror de los traidores,
pueblo, pueblo eficaz, corazón y fusiles,
corazón y fusiles, adelante.
Fotógrafos, mineros, ferroviarios, hermanos
del carbón y la piedra, parientes del martillo,
bosque, fiesta de alegres disparos, adelante,
guerrilleros, mayores, sargentos, comisarios políticos,
aviadores del pueblo, combatientes nocturnos,
combatientes marinos, adelante:
frente a vosotros
no hay más que una mortal cadena, un agujero
de podridos pescados: adelante!
no hay allí sino muertos moribundos,
pantanos de terrible pus sangrienta,
no hay enemigos; adelante, España,
adelante, campanas populares,
adelante, regiones de manzana,
adelante, estandartes cereales,
adelante, mayúsculos del fuego,
porque en la lucha, en la ola, en la pradera,
en la montaña, en el crepúsculo cargado de acre aroma,
lleváis un nacimiento de permanencia, un hilo
de difícil dureza.
                    Mientras tanto,
raíz y guirnalda suben del silencio
para esperar la mineral victoria:
cada instrumento, cada rueda roja,
cada mango de sierra o penacho de arado,
cada extracción del suelo, cada temblor de sangre
quiere seguir tus pasos, Ejército del Pueblo:

in the light of the lightning, your good health,
onward, onward, onward, onward,
over the mines, over the cemeteries, facing the abominable
appetite of death, facing the bristling
terror of the traitors,
people, effective people, hearts and guns,
hearts and guns, onward.
Photographers, miners, railroadmen, brothers
of coal and stone, relatives of the hammer,
woods, festival of gay nonsense, onward,
guerrilla fighters, chiefs, sergeants, political commissars,
people's aviators, night fighters,
sea fighters, onward:
facing you
there is only a mortal chain, a hole
of rotten fish: onward!
there are only dying dead there,
swamps of terrible bloody pus,
there are no enemies; onward, Spain,
onward, people's bells,
onward, apple orchards,
onward, banners of the grain,
onward, giants of the fire,
because in the struggle, in the wave, in the meadow,
in the mountain, in the twilight laden with acrid smell,
you bear a lineage of permanence, a thread
of hard harshness.
                    Meanwhile,
root and garland rise from the silence
to await the mineral victory:
each instrument, each red wheel,
each mountain mango or plume of plough,
each product of the soil, each tremor of blood
wants to follow your steps, Army of the People:

tu luz organizada llega a los pobres hombres
olvidados, tu definida estrella
clava sus roncos rayos en la muerte
y establece los nuevos ojos de la esperanza.

your ordered light reaches poor forgotten
men, your sharp star
sinks its raucous rays into death
and establishes the new eyes of hope.

Pablo Neruda

RESIDENCE ON EARTH

Residencia en la tierra

**Translated by Donald D. Walsh,
with a new Introduction by Jim Harrison**

"*Residence on Earth* is one of those very rare poems you must drown in. You don't understand it in discursive terms, you experience it.... Neruda haunts our bodies on an actual earth with the same power that Rilke haunts the more solitary aspects of our minds."

—Jim Harrison, from the Introduction

Residence on Earth (*Residencia en la tierra*) is widely regarded as Pablo Neruda's most influential work, a tempestuous ocean that became "a revolution...a classic by which masterpieces are judged" (*Review*). "In *Residence on Earth*," wrote Amado Alonso, "the tornado of fury will no longer pass without lingering, because it will be identified with Neruda's heart."

Written in the span of two decades (1925-1945), beginning when Neruda was twenty-one, *Residence on Earth* was originally published in Spanish in three successive volumes (1933, 1935, 1947). Most of these poems were penned when Neruda was a self-exiled diplomat in isolated regions of South Asia.

ISBN 0-8112-1581-4

Pablo Neruda

THE CAPTAIN'S VERSES
Los versos del Capitán

Translated by Donald D. Walsh

Matilde and I took refuge in our love....It was the first time we had lived together in the same house. In that place of intoxicating beauty, our love grew steadily. We could never again live apart. There I finished The Captain's Verses, *a book of love, passionate but also painful.... My love for Matilde, homesickness for Chile, passion for social consciousness fill the pages of this book that went through many editions without its author's name.*

—Pablo Neruda

Pablo Neruda finished writing *The Captain's Verses* (*Los versos del Capitán*) in 1952 while in exile on the island of Capri—the paradisal setting of the blockbuster film, *Il postino* (*The Postman*) that centers around this period of Neruda's life. Surrounded by the sea, sun, and the natural splendor of a thousand orchards and vineyards, Neruda addressed these poems of love, ecstasy, devotion, and fury to his lover, Matilde Urrutia, the one "with the fire / of an unchained meteor."

"It is difficult to find an analogue for the sustained passion and gentleness communicated in this absolutely stunning apotheosis of the poetry of sexual love....Neruda comes closest to the exultation of the Song of Solomon....Matilde Urrutia deserves to enter history in the company of Petrarch's Laura and Dante's Beatrice."

—*Library Journal*

ISBN 0-8112-1580-6

Nicanor Parra

ANTIPOEMS
How to look better and feel great

Antitranslation by Liz Werner

"One of the great names in the literature of our language."
—Pablo Neruda

"A poet with all the authority of a master."
—Mark Strand, *The New York Times Book Review*

"Real seriousness," Nicanor Parra, the antipoet of Chile, has said, rests in "the comic." And read in that light, this newest collection of his work is very serious indeed. It is an abundant offering of his signature mocking humor, subverting received conventions and pretensions in both poetry and everyday life, public and private, ingeniously and wittily rendered into English in an excellent antitranslation (the word is Parra's) by Liz Werner, who has lived and studied in Valparaìso, Chile, where she worked closely with Nicanor Parra in preparing this book.

"Liz Werner, the 'antitranslator,' has done a remarkable job of capturing the profoundly antic and deadly serious tone of Nicanor Parra's antipoetry. If you expect the staid reflections of an elder poet, you've come to the wrong book. Parra is as vital, and funny, and confounding as ever."
—Edith Grossman

ISBN 0-8112-1597-0

Federico García Lorca

SELECTED POEMS

With a new Introduction by W.S. Merwin

Edited, with a Preface, by Francisco García Lorca and Donald Allen

"What a poet! I have never seen grace and genius, a winged heart and a crystalline waterfall, come together in anyone else as they did in him. Federico García Lorca was the extravagant "duende," his was a magnetic joyfulness that generated a zest for life in his heart and radiated it like a planet."

—Pablo Neruda

The Selected Poems of Federico García Lorca has been the classic collection of Lorca's poems for generations of American readers. The translators of this selection—as diverse as Stephen Spender, Langston Hughes, Ben Belitt, William Jay Smith, and W.S. Merwin—have produced English versions which catch the spirit and intensity of the originals. Chosen from each of his original volumes as well as from posthumously published poems, this is a compilation of Lorca's very best.

This bilingual edition—original Spanish text facing the English text—is reissued with an Introduction by Pulitzer Prize-winning American poet, teacher, and translator W. S. Merwin, who says of Lorca: "What he wrote in his short life made it impossible to imagine the poetry not only of Spain and the Spanish language everywhere but of the whole Western world, since then, without him."

ISBN 0-8112-1622-5

Homero Aridjis

EYES TO SEE OTHERWISE

Ojos de otro mirar / SELECTED POEMS

Edited by Betty Ferber and George McWhirter

"Homero Aridjis's poems open a door into the light."
—Seamus Heaney

"Homero Aridjis [is] a poet of great vitality and originality."
—W.S. Merwin

Eyes to See Otherwise is the first extensive selection of poems by leading Mexican poet Homero Aridjis to appear in English. The range and quality of the translations, by some of America's finest poets, mark the centrality of his work on the map of modern poetry. He is, in the words of translator George McWhirter, "a troubadour of love for lost environments, a voice in the wilderness of Mexico City and Mexico."

Included in this selection are poems by Aridjis evoking his own life, present and past, his memories always sticking close to his birthplace Contepec, where, on Altamirano Hill, the Monarch butterflies arrive each year. This long awaited *Selected Poems* enables the reader to witness the poetic and personal evolution of this "visionary poet of lyrical bliss, crystalline concentrations and infinite spaces" (Kenneth Rexroth).

ISBN 0-8112-1509-1

THE NEW DIRECTIONS *Bibelots*

JORGE LUIS BORGES • EVERYTHING AND NOTHING

KAY BOYLE • THE CRAZY HUNTER

H.D. • KORA AND KA

SHUSAKU ENDO • FIVE BY ENDO

RONALD FIRBANK • CAPRICE

F. SCOTT FITZGERALD • THE JAZZ AGE

GUSTAVE FLAUBERT • A SIMPLE HEART

JOHN OF PATMOS • THE APOCALYPSE

FEDERICO GARCÍA LORCA • IN SEARCH OF DUENDE

THOMAS MERTON • THOUGHTS ON THE EAST

HENRY MILLER • A DEVIL IN PARADISE

YUKIO MISHIMA • PATRIOTISM

OCTAVIO PAZ • A TALE OF TWO GARDENS

VICTOR PELEVIN • 4 BY PELEVIN

EZRA POUND • DIPTYCH ROME-LONDON

WILLIAM SAROYAN • FRESNO STORIES

DELMORE SCHWARTZ • SCREENO

GARRY SNYDER • LOOK OUT

MURIEL SPARK • THE ABBESS OF CREWE
THE DRIVER'S SEAT

DYLAN THOMAS • EIGHT STORIES

TENN   S OF

WIL   HAT